PENGUIN BOOKS

THE LIFE AND TIMES OF MAUDIE LITTLEHAMPTON

Osbert Lancaster was born in 1908 and educated at Charterhouse and Lincoln College, Oxford. In 1939 he joined the *Daily Express* as a cartoonist, and between 1940 and 1947 he worked in the News Department of the Foreign Office, was attached to the British Embassy in Athens and was Sydney Jones Lecturer in Art at Liverpool University. Since 1969 he has been an Adviser to the G.L.C. Historic Buildings Board and he is a Governor of King Edward VII School, King's Lynn. An Hon.D.Lit. of the universities of Birmingham, Newcastle upon Tyne, St Andrews and Oxford, he is a Fellow of University College, London, and an Honorary Fellow of the Royal Institute of British Architects. He was awarded the C.B.E. in 1953 and knighted in 1975.

Osbert Lancaster has designed theatre décors for productions at Sadler's Wells, Covent Garden and Glyndebourne. His publications include *Pillar to Post*, *Homes Sweet Homes*, *Classical Landscape with Figures*, *The Saracen's Head*, *Facades and Faces*, *A Cartoon History of Architecture*, two volumes of auto-biography *(All Done From Memory* and *With an Eye to the Future)*, *The Little-hampton Bequest*, *The Pleasure Garden* (with his wife Anne Scott-James) and *Scene Changes*.

15

OSBERT LANCASTER

THE LIFE AND TIMES OF MAUDIE LITTLEHAMPTON

SELECTED BY GERALDINE COOK

INTRODUCED BY JOHN JULIUS NORWICH

PENGUIN BOOKS

Penguin Books Ltd, Harmondsworth, Middlesex, England
Penguin Books, 625 Madison Avenue, New York, New York 10022, U.S.A.
Penguin Books Australia Ltd, Ringwood, Victoria, Australia
Penguin Books Canada Ltd, 2801 John Street, Markham, Ontario, Canada L3R 1B4
Penguin Books (N.Z.) Ltd, 182-190 Wairau Road, Auckland 10, New Zealand

This selection first published simultaneously by Penguin Books and John Murray (Publishers) Ltd 1982

Made and printed in Great Britain
by Butler & Tanner Ltd,
Frome and London
Set in Garamond Light

INTRODUCTION

by John Julius Norwich

Osbert Lancaster was the best thing that ever happened to the *Daily Express*. Having contributed his first cartoon in the thirties, he continued – with a short interruption towards the end of the Second World War – into the eighties, maintaining throughout that period a standard of excellence that left us all flabbergasted. 'How on earth does he keep it up?' we asked ourselves, morning after morning; but we never received a satisfactory reply.

What was it that caused tens of thousands of respectable, well-balanced Englishmen to choke, several times a week, over their breakfast coffee or to sit, shoulders shaking, in their commuter carriages, praying for invisibility? This is perhaps a slightly easier question to answer. It was, I think, not the quality of the joke itself, hilarious as it might be; nor the brilliance of the draughts-manship, with its fiendish accuracy of observation; nor even the up-to-the-minute topicality of the subject which, it often seemed, could have been achieved only by clairvoyance. Rather was it the fusion of all three elements, which produced, chemically speaking, not a mixture but a compound, a whole that was greater far than the sum of its parts – a single, self-contained, unified work of art.

Osbert Lancaster performed this miracle not once but several thousand times – usually five times a week. In doing so, he gave a new dimension to the political cartoon. His style was utterly his own. It was not allegorical, in the manner of his Beaverbrook predecessors Strube and David Low; three of his rare ventures into this genre – which is now virtually moribund in this country, though still vigorous in America – are reproduced in this book, but do not show him really at his ease. It was not packed with extraneous, almost Breughelian incident in the manner of his colleague Carl Giles, who joined the *Express* four years after him. On the contrary – and herein, perhaps, lay its great individuality – it was unashamedly upper class. It was firmly rooted in Mayfair, Belgravia and St James's, seen from the inside. Thus, though Maudie and Willy Littlehampton and their friends are ceaselessly mocked, the mockery is always gentle, often affectionate and occasionally even tinged with admiration. Maudie may have her ridiculous side, but she possesses all the biting wit of her creator, for whom she frequently serves as a mouthpiece. The shafts she delivers have far more merciless barbs than those she receives.

Her only weapon, however, is her tongue; Osbert has his pencil as well, and one of the subsidiary pleasures of this book is that it enables us to follow the steady development of his technique through the early years of his work for the *Express* until – around 1950 as I see it – he had evolved that style, keen as a Toledo blade, in which every line carried its own built-in charge of wit. Facial expression has always been an obvious *forte* – my own particular favourites are those of the Lord Mayor and his coachman of November 1950 – but so are bodily attitudes (look at the two contributions for June 1956) and, above all, fashions. What a standby those must have been: whenever, on his arrival at the *Express* office around tea-time, a quick ruffle through the tapes would yield no inspiration for the next morning's cartoon, he could always fall back on the vagaries of *haute couture*. It was a theme that never let him down.

In his portrayal of foreigners, too, that extraordinary perception of his assured him a bull's-eye every time. German generals, French bohemians, Italian *papagalli*, intense Americans, orientals various – with all of them his touch is as certain as it is with his own compatriots, the formidable ladies in uniform or, in the unforgettable phrase of Nathaniel Gubbins, the 'witty worm friends' propping up the bar in White's.' Of all the humourists that this (or indeed any other) country has produced, only Peter Ustinov and Peter Sellers have, in their very different fields, a comparable deadliness of aim. Except when these foreigners are talking among themselves, one notices that they very seldom actually *make* the jokes; if an Englishman or Englishwoman is present, it is he or she who almost invariably delivers the punch-line. But that is as it should be: the Lancaster humour is itself quintessentially English, and the words which ring so true when spoken by Lady Littlehampton, Aunt Ethel or Canon Fontwater would sound strange indeed on the lips of Gigi Pernod-Framboise, let alone Mrs Rajagojollibarmi.

Much thought was given to those words. It was not Osbert's way, as with so many of his fellows, to pare his captions down to an absolute minimum. He was not afraid to spread himself when he felt that the occasion required it; after all, upper-class conversation has never been noted for its verbal economy, and accuracy always came first. But what could be shorter, or more telling, than the single word beneath that little masterpiece of 23 June 1964? And, surely, no other cartoonist – with the possible exception of the very different James Thurber – could have found so perfect a distillation of a joke as the words 'Tell me dear, is Zbigniew Brzezinski them or us?'

Newspapers are, by definition, ephemeral and Osbert has moved into his richly deserved retirement, but this book, together with the annual collections with which he and Mr Murray have regularly regaled us over the years, has ensured the survival of one of the very greatest comic achievements of our time – which also happens to be a deeply perceptive commentary of our changing habits and attitudes. Social historians in the next century will bless Osbert Lancaster as we have done in ours – while, as with us, the tears of laughter run down their faces.

THE LIFE AND TIMES OF MAUDIE LITTLEHAMPTON

THE FORTIES

Although Osbert Lancaster's very first cartoon in the *Daily Express*, published in January 1939, was only the mildest of satires directed against town planners, the clouds were gathering fast. On 23 August Hitler and Stalin signed a Non-Aggression Pact (less than two years before Germany invaded Russia) and on 3 September war was declared. Osbert found himself with almost as many targets as Bomber Command. In the early days there were invasion fears, evacuees, rationing, travel restrictions (*Is Your Journey Really Necessary?*), the multiple manifestations of Home Security (*Careless Talk Costs Lives*) and the for him endlessly entertaining phenomenon – it was to remain a favourite subject for the next forty years – of Women in Uniform. Later came the awkwardnesses of the unexpected Soviet alliance, the arrival of the Italian prisoners of war to work on the land and – another godsend to a cartoonist – the extension of the war to North Africa, visited with increasing frequency by the Prime Minister.

When the war ended, Osbert was on attachment to the British Embassy in Athens; but on his return in 1946 he found the atmosphere of wartime England surprisingly little changed. Shortages and restrictions appeared unaffected by the Peace; the rationing of bread continued till 1948, that of clothes till 1949. Fuel, too, continued in short supply. Labour was in; the workers, more and more often, were out. But there were compensations. Television was resumed – to an audience of less than 12,000 – and in 1948 the arrival in England of M. Dior's New Look re-awoke the country to the pleasures and tyrannies of Fashion. With the slow return of more affluent days the cartoons were able to acquire a new dimension and – already dressed, Athena-like, to kill – Maudie Littlehampton was born.

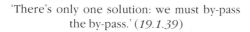

'There's only one solution: we must by-pass the by-pass.' (*19.1.39*)

'Mark my words, the Government are over-doing these air-raid rehearsals; one of these days there'll be a real raid and no one will believe it.' (*6.6.39*)

'I tell you frankly – if this session is prolonged over Goodwood it'll only give Hitler an undue sense of his own importance.' (*25.7.39*)

(*25.8.39*)

'The Government don't appear to realise that if they cut our profits now we shan't be in a position to buy peerages when the war's over.' (*22.6.39*)

'Honestly, Madam, do I *look* like an evacuated child?' (*11.1.40*)

'After all, if Hitler is such a cad as to invade us over Whitsun, our place is obviously with our constituents.' (*10.5.40*)

'It may sound caddish, Sir George, but 'pon my word I don't care if it is the breeding season.' (*1939/40*)

'The Doctor says it's a sort of birth-mark.'
(*1939/40*)

'Anybody here from M.I.5. . . Anybody here
from M.I.5?' (*28.3.40*)

'When he said he was a Yorkshire terrier on his mother's side, I said: "You tell that to M.I.5."' (*1.6.40*)

'Shall we join the gentlemen?' (*26.6.40*)

'. . . a stranger from overseas will shortly effect a big change in your position . . .' (*12.11.40*)

'Listen! I've found a man who can make the Internationale sound just like "Home, Sweet Home".' (*17.7.41*)

'Which are we, Carruthers – workers, peasants or intellectuals?' (*18.7.41*)

'Your grandfather wore it at Rorke's Drift. Gird it on and never let it leave your side!' (*10.1.42*)

'I dessay it's different in the Isle o' Capri, but in Shepton Mallet we don't 'ave no siesta hour.' (*19.1.42*)

'I repeat, Sir, the Japs are no sportsmen – it's always been clearly understood that these jungles are strictly inpenetrable.' (*20.1.42*)

'Tell me, Achmed, what shall I do? My first wife is pro-Darlan, my second is pro-de Gaulle and all the rest want to go to England to join the Home Guard!!' (*15.12.42*)

'Well, if it isn't Widow Fatima, who is it? Just tell me that.' (*1942/3*)

'The official military spokesman stated in Berlin today that the war in the East has now entered a more mobile phase.' (*9.1.43*)

'It was all very well for Balaam – his ass didn't keep on saying "Is your journey really necessary?"' (*25.1.43*)

'Don't come worrying us about this war when
we're so busy on plans for the next.' (*25.7.43*)

'Breeding will tell, Herr Graf – *he* didn't
outstay his welcome.' (*24.7.44*)

23

'He who rides on a tiger can never dismount.' – *Chinese proverb* (13.2.44)

'Oh, look, sir – "the hounds of spring are on winter's traces".' (*15.3.44*)

'At the thard stroke eet will be the eleventh hour precaisely!' (*10.5.44*)

'Sir Louis is a little despondent this morning – last night he lost the whole of his month's sweet coupons on a single rubber.' (*1.3.43*)

'I'm not denying that there may be a split in the German High Command. All I say is that G.O.C. Pas de Calais seems to be fanatically loyal.' (*22.7.44*)

'I hope, Wainscote, you'll be a little more careful than you were in 1918. Next time we don't want to find them full of moth again.' (*13.9.44*)

'Excuse me, Canon, but I rather think you've liberated my matches.' (*7.10.44*)

'Now if I were the guy handling this situation, I'd let that poor little black dawg right off his lead.'
(*11.8.46*)

Mr Zilliacus: 'If you would only call down that whacking great lion, this poor little fellow could get off quite easily.' (*27.10.46*)

'Except for 32 squatters, 16 typists left behind by the Ministry of Food, an escaped P.O.W. and some bats, the 'ole place is as silent as the grave.' (*13.9.46*)

'It's a funny thing, but only last night my wife was saying she wondered if there was any opening for her on the Third Programme.' (*13.12.46*)

'Brightly shone the moon that night,
Tho' the frost was cruel,
Extra brightly just to spite
The Minister of Fue-oo-el.'
(*24.12.46*)

'One can't even put one's head in a gas-oven with the smallest prospect of success.'
(*31.1.47*)

'My subject this afternoon is "Some recent developments in high-tension molecular fission and their application to modern industry".' (*8.2.47*)

'Hilda! Why don't *we*? (*29.3.47*)

'Are you proposing to come in to lunch or do you expect me to bring you some sandwiches on the course?' (*17.5.47*)

'If you ask me, Maudie Littlehampton is wearing one of her husband's old parachutes.' (*18.6.47*)

'If young Worplesdon goes on much more about "the New Look" there's going to be dirty work after evensong.' (*9.1.48*)

'As I told Maudie Littlehampton, one would never *dream* of dressing up like this if one didn't think one was helping the export drive.' (*24.1.48*)

'Salisbury can compromise if he likes, but I shall stop at nothing to defend my rights – even if it means going up to London to do it.' (*6.2.48*)

'Carissima mia, either you supporta da Musicians' Union or I wrecka your encore. See?' (*5.3.48*)

'Well, dear, as that's going to be the last cab we shall see for a long, long time, you'd better make sure we get it.' (*17.7.48*)

'Turn left where it says "No cigarettes", keep straight on past wot used to be the petrol pump till you sees a notice saying "No admittance by order of the War Office", and that's the old Elizabethan Manor 'ouse.' (*25.8.48*)

'Darling, how does one entertain Americans? . . . If one gives them Spam and doesn't change, we're a down-at-heel, C3 nation, dying of malnutrition, while if one blows the week's meat ration and wears a new frock one's shamelessly abusing Marshall aid!'
(*12.11.48*)

' . . . for the "Coach and Horses" read "The Nationalised Transport Workers"; for "The Marquis of Granby" read "The Regional Commissioner"; for "The Crown" read "The State"; for "The Goat and Compasses" read "The New Statesman and Nation" . . . '
(*16.12.48*)

'Before taking you over to the theatre for tonight's performance of "The Beggar's Opera", I want you to try to imagine that we are back in 18th-century London, a London infested with highwaymen and footpads, and not a single policeman –' (*4.1.49*)

'Once and for all, Alfred, will you please realise it's practically no comfort to me to be told "We've got something far, far nastier up our sleeves." ' (*24.9.49*)

THE FIFTIES

The fifties began with the Korean War; for some years already the Russians had taken the place of the Germans in the public mind. Doggedly, however, plans continued for the Festival of Britain, designed to show that anything the Prince Consort could do in 1851 we could do better a century later. 'Don't make fun of the Festival,' Noël Coward implored us, '*Don't* make fun of the Fair'; but Osbert did, repeatedly. Another favourite target was Dr Hewlett Johnson, the 'Red Dean' of Canterbury. In the Lancaster game calendar, it has always been open season for ecclesiastics, and the unfortunate incident when, in January 1951, an outraged member kicked Mr Aneurin Bevan down the steps of White's Club was clearly not an opportunity to be missed.

Those who had been less than impressed by the scientific progress demonstrated by the Festival found more convincing proof in the development of the hydrogen bomb, first exploded by the Americans in 1952, and by the Russians a year later. But the Coronation cheered everyone up – and, incidentally, gave a considerable boost to the sales of television sets, though Lady Littlehampton and her friends would still never have admitted to actually *owning* one. Maudie's time was in any case increasingly taken up by her daughter Jennifer, who made her long-awaited *début* in 1955. Suez, in the following year, was the next excitement – the Arabs we had known so well during the war, selling filthy postcards at Port Said, didn't look a day older – and kept Osbert happy well into 1957. When at last the dust settled, there was always Fashion to fall back on; his contribution of 29 May 1958 still has me laughing out loud.

'Sometimes I can't help wondering just how long it'll be before rather similar stories start appearing in the Martian Press.' (*28.1.50*)

'Darling, doesn't it strike you as rather sinister that so far nobody seems to be making any effort to attract the Upper-Class vote?' (*30.1.50*)

'Oh, we're enjoying every minute of it – he's bitten the Tory, been sick over the Socialist and now I can hardly wait to see what he's going to do to the Liberal!' (*20.2.50*)

'Why, your Excellency, I promise you I've been looking forward to a long, cosy chat ever since my husband told me the Diplomatic Corps have practically *unlimited* petrol!' (*7.3.50*)

'How right you were, dear, when you said it had been just like a pre-war weekend!' (*27.6.50*)

'Lady Littlehampton sends her love and please do you think the Russians will move before Goodwood?' (*30.6.50*)

'Oh dear, I'm afraid things are getting really serious, Maudie Littlehampton's got that old 1939 of-course-my-lips-are-sealed-but-I'm-really-working-for-M.I.5 look.' (*19.7.50*)

'No, no, Therese, your price is too high – I cannot betray the plans of my country's Festival!!' (*20.10.50*)

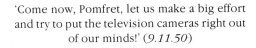

'Come now, Pomfret, let us make a big effort and try to put the television cameras right out of our minds!' (*9.11.50*)

'How times have changed! When I first joined the Foreign Office it was we who started wars and the military who finished 'em!' (*29.11.50*)

'Have a care, Fontwater! – we're not in
White's!' (*29.1.51*)

'Darling, just point me out the Palace of
Groundnuts and the Gambia Egg Pavilion.'
(*28.4.51*)

'But Willy darling, if it's bad form to make jokes about Americans, and tactless to ask diplomats where they're going for their holidays, and breach of privilege to criticise the Government, what on earth is one going to talk about?!' (*20.6.51*)

'Now why on earth, darling, should you think it's either Burgess or Maclean? For all you know it's just as likely to be our host.' (*19.7.51*)

'Please, exactly which building is it that is going to be sent to Coventry and turned into the new cathedral when the exhibition's over?' (*27.9.51*)

'Wotcher mean – I look like a floating vote?' (*22.10.51*)

'I suppose if I'd told you it was by Sartre you'd have thought it wonderful!' (*20.12.51*)

'Another time perhaps you'll deign to listen when I tell you there's a zebra crossing!!' (*21.12.51*)

'Now is the time for all good men to come to the aid of Apartheid. Heil Malan!' (*24.3.52*)

'But Willy, you old stupid, if Gigi Pernod-Framboise gives me the money in francs and I lose it back to her at Canasta in pounds, Mr Butler can't possibly object.' (*31.7.52*)

'Half measures are no good, we must force the Government to close the museums entirely – they're a gross waste of public money and compete unfairly with sponsored television!' (16.7.52)

'To think, my dear Littlehampton, that these are the fellows who have the nerve to talk about reforming the Lords.' (1.8.52)

'Better come away now, dear – you know how madly secretive primitive peoples always are about their tribal magic.' (4.10.52)

'Willy, darling, come and see how I'm going to look in the Abbey!' (3.6.53)

' – and here is Leonardo's supreme master-piece – the Mona Lisa!! Are you, too, afraid to open your mouth when you smile?' (*20.6.53*)

'Penny for the guy?' (*24.10.53*)

'Well, if only you'd get yourself a job I shouldn't have to make these annual concessions to bourgeois prejudice!!' (*12.12.53*)

'I suppose it's all really a desperate effort to try to attract a better class of Member!' (*17.2.54*)

'May I remind you, Lady Littlehampton, that you were not asked to tell the panel what they could do with the object, but what it is!' (23.2.54)

'Considering all things, darling, I've come to the conclusion that smoking's worth the risk.' (26.3.54)

'I never thought the day would come when I would look to the Budget for light, escapist reading!' (6.4.54)

'If we really want to rearm Germany, what's wrong with the old system of forbidding her to do it and looking terribly, terribly surprised when she does?' (29.9.54)

'My, my, Mr Bickersteth, aren't you the lucky one!!' (*29.12.54*)

Lady Littlehampton's only daughter Jennifer, one of the loveliest of the year's debutantes, leaving the Palace yesterday after her presentation. (*4.3.55*)

' – and don't forget what I said about not getting plastered before the Season's properly started!' (*8.3.55*)

'I dare say Gina Lollobrigida did wear one just like it but Gina Lollobrigida wasn't going to a quiet little dinner dance at the Tetlock-Smythes.' (*10.3.55*)

'Ernesto's *not* a penniless ice-creamer! He comes of a very ancient Roman family and owns half the Espressos in Knightsbridge!!' (*22.3.55*)

'For Heaven's sake, child, do at least try and *look* as though you're enjoying yourself!' (*29.4.55*)

'Mummy darling, guess what? – that's me!!'
(*30.4.55*)

'Oh, yes, the children are growing up fast –
why, Torquil's just got his first endorsement
and Jennifer passed out at Queen Charlotte's
ball!' (*11.5.55*)

'You know, darling, I'm just a teeny bit worried about Jennifer these days – she seems to get so easily overtired.' (*29.6.55*)

'Darling Mummy,
Do you remember your saying that the only way really to learn French is to live in a family? . . .' (*20.8.55*)

'Excuse me, but why on earth did you ever give up burning scientists as witches?' (*2.9.55*)

'Thank you, I know all about the importance of mother-love, but if you don't stop pinching my nylons you're going to feel more emotionally insecure and unwanted than you've ever felt in your life!!' (*14.9.55*)

'Darling, why is it called the *Secret* Service?'
(27.9.55)

'Poor Willy's very low! He says he does think
that they might at least have waited to launch
coronary thrombosis until he'd got over
worrying about smoker's lung!' (6.10.55)

'I *do* wish the P.M. would make up his mind about the Cabinet reshuffle – the strain of not knowing whom to drop and whom to take up is almost killing me!' (*14.10.55*)

'All right, darling, if I let you have the new Graham Greene for three pairs of nylons not your size, will you take the Brahms Third Symphony in part exchange for that large bottle of Chanel No. 5?' (*29.12.55*)

'It's all very well the P.M. saying we'll stand by our friends in the Middle East, but what on earth makes him think we've still got any friends in the Middle East?' (*9.3.56*)

'Oh, to hell with Nancy Mitford! What I always say is – if it's *me* it's U!' (*1.5.56*)

'Mr Van Hamburger, will you please realise, once and for all, that there are certain British assets which will for ever remain beyond the reach of dollar-imperialism!!' (*16.6.56*)

'Lady Littlehampton?' (*20.6.56*)

'Let me recall the warning I gave when your lordships decided to abolish the rack. "This," I said, "is the thin end of the wedge"!' (*11.7.56*)

'I wonder if Colonel Nasser has ever seen a nationalised canal?' (*8.8.56*)

'Your poor uncle is dreadfully depressed – he keeps on referring to the Canal as some creek or other and says we are right up it without a paddle!' (*16.8.56*)

'Unfortunately, that's not the only thing he's stepped in!' (*3.1.57*)

'Darling, the First Lesson was sheer bliss – all about what happened to the Egyptians when there wasn't any United Nations!!' (*19.2.57*)

'Now there's a pair of knees that haven't changed a bit!' (*12.2.58*)

'My dear·Willy, if only you weren't so hopelessly out of touch you wouldn't go leaping
to ridiculous conclusions!' (*29.5.58*)

'Agoraphobia, dear, means fear of open
spaces and all the No. 9's have got it badly.'
(*2.12.59*)

THE SIXTIES

The Space Age had begun. Laika, the world's most popular dog since Rin-Tin-Tin, was rocketed into space by the Russians and retrieved none the worse for her experience – to be followed shortly afterwards by Major Yuri Gagarin. The next major barrier to be overcome was the English Channel: Mr Edward Heath, Lord Privy Seal under Harold Macmillan, began his eleven-year task of getting us into the Common Market. Nearer home, the great Picasso Exhibition at the Tate opened in the summer of 1960; the death of Sir Alfred Munnings less than a year earlier was much regretted.

Spies, largely forgotten since the days of Burgess and Maclean, came back into the news. The mole Gordon Lonsdale was found to have burrowed deep into the recesses of the Admiralty; shortly afterwards it was the turn of the Foreign Office again with George Blake – whose trial, however, fortunately coincided with the arrival of Rudolf Nureyev to prove that some people at least liked things better over here. The sexual revolution was also upon us: the seeds sown by the Wolfenden Report were yielding a rich harvest – which Osbert, as usual, was not slow to reap. Meanwhile, London had started to swing: the cartoons charted the course of the phenomenon from the Beatles to the days of the Hippies and Flower Power, delighting as wickedly as ever in the accompanying developments on the sartorial scene: the Mini, the Maxi, the Topless and all those breathtaking improbabilities subsumed in the word GEAR. Skyscrapers meanwhile rose higher and higher – though one of them, Ronan Point, came crashing down.

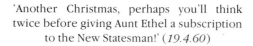

'Another Christmas, perhaps you'll think twice before giving Aunt Ethel a subscription to the New Statesman!' (*19.4.60*)

'Mummy's blissfully happy. She's making a list of the first people she'd like to see sent into orbit.' (*1.6.60*)

'What I particularly admired about the debate was the way that every speaker managed to give the impression that he personally had never met a homosexual in his life.' (*1.7.60*)

'If it hadn't been for the fact that the bar's in here I should never have got your father past the "Blue Period".' (*7.7.60*)

'It's the Foreign Office – they want to know whether you can possibly remember that frightfully funny story you told them at the time of Burgess and Maclean?' (*23.3.61*)

'Am I correct in assuming that membership of the Common Market will entitle this country to the free and unrestricted use of the guillotine?' (*10.10.61*)

'Maud dear, pray explain to me exactly what it is out of which dear Prince Philip is so eager that we should all take our fingers.' (*19.10.61*)

'I hope you've realised, Miss Flatiron, that if Mr Heath has his way you'll soon be finding yourself in direct competition with Balenciaga and Chanel.' (*28.11.61*)

'It never ceases to astonish me the amount of time those hearty, outdoor hunting types always seem to manage to spend indoors.'
(*16.12.61*)

'Of course, without a saliva test one can't be absolutely sure, but I think I've been doped.'
(*19.6.62*)

'Well, dear, the principal difference as far as I can see is this – a DEfensive weapon is one with my finger on the trigger, an OFfensive weapon is one with yours.' (*26.10.62*)

'I'm sorry, Jasper, but if staying out of Europe means we're going to get a little less of "Brecht, Brecht, Brecht," I'm all for it!' (*1.2.63*)

'But, Charles, this is so sudden!' (*5.2.63*)

'Tell me, Canon, are you as bored with Pre-marital Intercourse as I am?' (*23.2.63*)

'Is that the one we swopped for Burgess?'
(*19.3.63*)

'The extraordinary thing is that one never seems to meet any of the remaining two-thirds!' (*1.5.63*)

' – and two and a quarter breathtaking hours to London Airport.' (*9.10.63*)

'Pray God it's not A. L. Rowse!!!' (*13.11.63*)

'Those whom Sir Keith Joseph hath joined together let no man put asunder!' (*3.1.64*)

'The Brothers Karamazov, I presume!?' (*4.1.64*)

'It is my duty to tell you, Monsignor Canteloupe, that there is a widespread feeling in the club that your attitude toward umbrellas is too ecumenical by half!' (*7.1.64*)

'Surprise! Surprise!! Snow in January!!!' (*14.1.64*)

'Sure, Father, an' I thought it was just an aspirin.' (*8.5.64*)

'What I can never understand, Excellency, is how on earth anyone ever decides whether a diplomat is drugged or not.' (*9.5.64*)

'But, Colonel, they haven't *got* any whites of their eyes!' (*20.5.64*)

'For heaven's sake, Willy, please stop wondering whether they're open yet and just remember that you're nearer God's heart in a garden than anywhere else on earth!' (*27.5.64*)

'Papa!!!' (*23.6.64*)

'I do think it's most terribly bad luck that no one seems able to think up any remotely convincing sexual smear to brighten up the Liberal image.' (*8.10.64*)

'But, mummy darling, it's me! Your daughter!!
Jennifer!!!' (*23.10.65*)

'You realise, of course, that the Speech does
not reflect the Sovereign's personal views,
and that the whole thing has been written out
for her by Baldwin?' (*10.11.65*)

'You will doubtless be glad to know, Maxwell, that I have just submitted your request for a rise to the Prices and Incomes Board.' (*12.3.66*)

'Tell me, dear child, which particular horse did you put your skirt on?' (*16.6.66*)

' 'Have you heard about poor Alison? My dear, she was swooped on by one of Mr Wilson's young eagles!' (6.7.66)

'O come off it, doctor! I'm sure Hippocrates wouldn't mind a bit your telling me whether Poppy Mountpleasant's ulcers are partly psychosomatic or entirely drink.' (8.7.66)

'Darling, lend me a hairpin.' (*8.10.66*)

'The last time *you* gave pussy the kiss of life she didn't draw a sober breath for three weeks.' (*11.10.66*)

'Well, well, Mrs Frogmarch, and how are the Flower People this fine morning?' (*29.9.67*)

'All over the country the grime, muddle and decay of our Victorian heritage is being replaced and the quality of urban life uplifted!' – Harold Wilson. (*5.10.67*)

'I take it that the "E" is silent, as in "MERDE".'
(*12.12.67*)

'You mark my words, Matron – it'll be cystitis
that keeps the old pot boiling this winter!'
(*22.12.67*)

'Honestly, darling, you can't – it's really *too* kinky!' (*29.12.67*)

'Tell me, dear, are you playing the second lead in *Hiawatha* or is it just a touch of ringworm?' (*19.3.68*)

'I bet whoever gets *your* liver won't wake up bright and smiling!' (*7.5.68*)

'Trust Aunt Ethel to make difficulties! She says she doesn't mind what we take her to on her birthday provided it's heterosexual and has a happy ending.' (*27.3.69*)

83

'That's St Paul's, that was!'
(*24.7.69*)

'How typical! Too little, too late!' (*31.10.69*)

'Oh no, we never have bomb outrages over here – our sky-flats fall down quite by themselves.' (*14.11.69*)

THE SEVENTIES

Violence was, quite literally, in the air. You could not board an aeroplane to anywhere without half expecting to end up in Cuba. In England, the days of affluence were over; effluence, on the other hand, seemed a good deal nearer home as we all got terribly concerned about what we had learnt to call the Environment. Maudie had largely renounced *haute couture*; like most of her friends, she tended to fall back on kaftans off the peg. The Arabs reappeared; no longer, however, in the casbahs of North Africa but in the more salubrious surroundings of Kensington and Chelsea. The Earl of Littlehampton, ageing appreciably, could still seek solace where he had always found it in the past, but with every budget his future looked bleaker.

For Osbert, too, there were compensations. Mrs Mary Whitehouse was one, Watergate another. But as the decade drew, surprisingly peacefully, to its close, he seemed to see little hope of improvement, and one suspects that Aunt Ethel's gloomy prognostication about the eighties was, in fact, his own.

'You remember that bomber we sold to the French for undercover resale to the Saudi Arabians for transfer to Biafra? Well, it got diverted to Israel and now it's been hijacked by Bernadette Devlin acting on behalf of the Welsh Nationalists.' (*17.1.70*)

'I'm sorry, m'lady, but I'm afraid his Grace is away on safari – right down the other end of the drive.' (*2.9.70*)

'Do you remember telling me that the trouble with the Arabs was that they were temperamentally incapable of organisation?' (*8.9.70*)

'As far as I'm concerned the sooner the British car industry gets into Europe and out of West Kensington the better.' (*10.10.70*)

'Steady on with the untreated effluent, Mousehole!' (*21.10.70*)

'My dear, I know for a fact that when they computerised the details of her private life the data-bank blew up.' (*21.11.70*)

'Mummy, darling, what *were* the Beatles?'
(*2.1.71*)

'But it's all so simple, m'lady! We just take away the number we first thought of, double it, and that gives us the price in decimals.'
(*5.1.71*)

'Ah, well, that's the way it goes – one day you're on the air, the next you're on the menu.' (*26.1.71*)

'Well, all we need now's some sackcloth!' (*18.2.71*)

'And don't pretend you don't know what
I mean by "environmental pollution".'
(*24.2.71*)

'How dare you tell my daughter I'm no longer
on the Pill?!' (*27.2.71*)

'Can't modern children learn *anything* by themselves?' (*20.4.71*)

'Will Mrs Bracegirdle, winner of the Mothers' Union Egg and Spoon Race, please come at once to the Red Cross tent for a saliva test.' (*15.8.72*)

'I say, Daphne, isn't it *super* about the new Laureate?!' (*11.10.72*)

'If you ask me, it's not the Russian winter that's going to fix Napoleon, but a good old English power strike.' (*24.10.72*)

'Don't be a foolish virgin – stock up now!'
(*27.10.72*)

'Until that wretched Mrs Whitehouse piped
up, your dear grandfather had quite forgotten
that he'd got a ding-a-ling.' (*30.11.72*)

'It may say it's budgie food, Judson, but these Fenians stick at nothing – open it in the servants' hall!' (*21.9.73*)

'How comes it that the Americans, with all their experience, always assassinate the wrong Presidents?' (*30.10.73*)

'More disasters! Boots have annexed Harrods
and the United Nations haven't lifted a finger.'
(*8.11.73*)

'To avoid disappointment I think I should
warn you that dear Freda's martinis are
definitely post-Budget.' (*4.4.74*)

'Don't get alarmed, Daddy darling, there's no question of wedding bells – it's just a social contract.' (*5.9.74*)

'Has the bidding started yet?' (*19.11.74*)

'Too late!' (*6.12.74*)

'I'm told that the trouble with Willie Hamilton is that he was once badly frightened by a corgi in his pram.' (*13.2.75*)

'After I told them that we brought fraternal greetings from the Freedom Fighters of SW1 they couldn't have been sweeter!' (*30.9.75*)

'Well, if Mrs Thatcher's the first woman Ted Heath's ever found himself opposed to, it explains a lot.' (*9.10.75*)

'Dear child, if there is one thing of which we do not need to be reminded it is "gunpowder, treason and plot".' (*6.11.75*)

'Now remember, darling, that we made a New Year resolution to keep an open mind about Mrs Thatcher.' (*6.1.76*)

'Poor little Suki's had a most terrible shock –
she was raped by a lesbian Great Dane in
Poodle drag!' (*12.2.76*)

'By the time the Presidential election's over
we shall be regretting that we ever said a
harsh word about the Olympic Games.'
(*12.8.76*)

'I'm sick of Samuel Palmer, how do you spell Modigliani?' (*25.8.76*)

'What are we playing for? Petrol or gin?' (*8.10.76*)

'But, Willy darling, why should you expect an unkind mention – you were never a close friend?' (*2.11.76*)

'Is it true that we all have to cut Prince Philip, and curtsy to Callaghan?' (*20.1.77*)

'Well – as far as I can make out what you lose upon the roundabouts you lose upon the swings.' (*30.3.77*)

'Just what we don't want – what we need is a bomb that wrecks the architecture and spares the inhabitants!' (*14.7.77*)

'Dear Mrs Rajagojollibarmi, if it weren't for the Race Relations Board I'd say you've revoked!' (*10.1.78*)

'If Ted and Maggie don't make it up soon everyone will start saying there's more to this than meets the eye!' (*15.2.78*)

'You mark my words, any minute now they'll discover that nuclear radiation is terribly good for us, and up will go the rates!' (*7.3.78*)

'Do you *really* want to know Leyland's balance sheet for 1980?' (*21.3.78*)

'How do babies come? Quite honestly, darling, granny's no longer one hundred per cent certain.' (*20.7.78*)

'Let's look on the bright side, dear – it might have been Daimler's.' (*26.9.78*)

'Why do so many of our public figures feel the need, in moments of crisis, to express themselves in hopelessly outdated slang?' (*8.11.78*)

'One can only hope that whoever did leak will come very high in the next Honours List!' (*1.3.79*)

'If only the Welsh had opted for independence!' (*13.3.79*)

'How often must I tell you not to call me "Comrade" in front of the electors!' (*11.4.79*)

"Ought we to tell him that *The Times* hasn't been published for seven months?' (*13.7.79*)

'I don't want to boast, but I don't think I've ever taken a tea-break in my life!' (*23.8.79*)

' . . . and what's thirty million down and nothing across in five letters?' (*23.10.79*)

'You mark my words! The Eighties will be worse – they always are!' (*20.12.79*)

'If you ask me, the Come to Britain campaign's been a dam' sight too successful!' (*18.1.80*)

'But what makes you think that Europe wants to get any closer to us?' (*20.3.80*)

'Tell me, dear, is Zbigniew Brzezinski them or us?' (*29.4.80*)

'Don't you start harassing me – I'm free, white and not on a yellow line!' (*1.7.80*)

'Does the Rev. Paisley have NO parish duties?!'
(*8.7.80*)

'Personally, I'm not putting all my eggs in one basket – I'm going to be a top executive AND a dolly-bird!' (*11.7.80*)

'If it's from Aunt Ethel and it ticks I wouldn't open it in here!' (*30.10.80*)

'Grandpa, how was it that during all those years in the Foreign Office you were never kidnapped?' (*20.1.81*)